Work

tends to ruin your day

This book is dedicated to my long-suffering work colleagues

First published in the United Kingdom in 2016 by
Portico
1 Gower Street
London
WC1E 6HD

An imprint of Pavilion Books Company Ltd

ISBN 978-1-91104-211-2

A CIP catalogue record for this book is available from the British Library.

10 9 8 7 6 5 4 3 2 1

Design: Suzanne Perkins/grafica
Reproduction by Mission Productions Ltd, Hong Kong
Printed and bound by Toppan Leefung Printing Ltd, China

This book can be ordered direct from the publisher at www.pavilionbooks.com

THE WIT AND WISDOM OF
Cath Tate

Work

tends to ruin your day

PORTICO

I love Mondays.

"I like work.
It fascinates me. I can sit
and look at it for hours."

"Just because I work here,
don't assume I *work* here."

Work's not bad but it does
tend to mess up your day.

"We don't need
to work,
we only do it for
the money."

"We always arrive late,
but we make up for it by
going home early."

The mind has an energy-saving feature.

It switches off the minute you get to work.

She had perfected the art of the all-day lunch hour.

"I love work. The gossip
is great and I can get my
online shopping done."

The trouble with
tidying your desk
is that…

∾

… you end up with a terrible mess in your desk drawer.

∽

"The best thing about my job is that my chair spins round."

"If I plan to do nothing,
and then I do nothing,
have I in fact then done
something?"

Nothing beats the satisfaction of crossing things off a list.

Only Robinson Crusoe got everything done by Friday.

"I'll do a lot of things for money but I draw the line at working."

"I'm a tax expert, book-keeper, psychologist, designer, dirty cup washer, economist, diplomat, trade fair stand builder, receptionist, production manager, IT expert, tea maker, advertising executive, statistician, sales manager, warehouse worker, dodgy email deleter.

I just run a small business."

⊙ ⊙ ⊙

Meetings.
A great
alternative to
work.

If you want to bury a project, set up a committee to look at the idea.

Avoid failure
by not trying to
do it in the first
place.

The first job of a boss is
to work out who to blame
when things go wrong.

"Unfortunately, shouting at my staff doesn't seem to work any more."

Those who think they know everything are really annoying for those of us who do know everything.

"It's not the work
I hate.
It's the people."

ANNUAL STAFF APPRAISAL

SUMMARY OF ACHIEVEMENT

TO DATE:

 2,346 mixed paperclips

AIMS AND OBJECTIVES:

4,000 paperclips, in neat rows,

by year end.

Team-building weekends apparently create a more productive work force.

"This quarter my sales figures were an inspiration to my colleagues."

"When I grow up I want to be a Health and Safety Officer."

"I shall be out of the office today due to illness. Absolutely nothing to do with my birthday, absolutely nothing at all."

In case of illness the company requires that you Get Better Immediately!

Computers are wonderful.
Whatever happens, no one
is to blame.

In the future
all problems will be solved
by technology.

In the future
all problems will be caused
by technology.

Never let a computer know you're in a hurry.

"Good morning, technical support, how may I help you?"

TROUBLESHOOTING

What to do when your printer is playing up.

"My phone has an app that rings and you can speak to people."

Your call may be monitored for staff entertainment purposes.

"After my bedtime story
I go online and hack into
people's computers."

Manure is like money.
It's useful spread around
evenly and stinks when a
few people have
great piles of it.

My company is so big that:

We tell people what
they want.

Our suppliers get paid
almost nothing.

We ignore local planning
regulations.

We move anywhere that wages
are rock-bottom.

We hide our profits offshore.

We screw up the environment.

We have a
green office to
show that we
care about the
environment.

Leaving the job? You don't believe there's anywhere better than here, do you?

"I've decided to give up the day job and concentrate on my music."

As a freelancer, you only have to *sound* dressed at 9.30 in the morning.

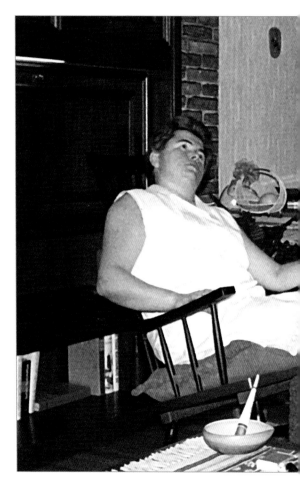

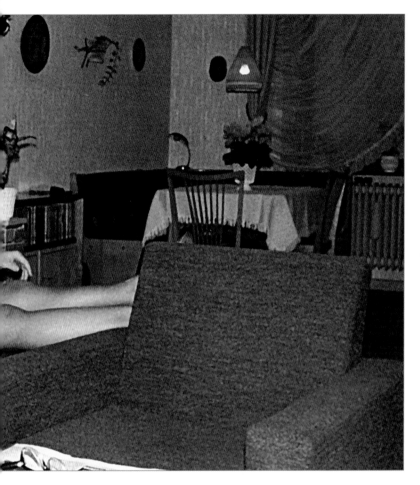

There's always something more interesting to do than fill in your tax return.

"Wake me up when the recession's over."

⚓

"I don't work.
I just wake,
feed, wash,
dress, untangle,
motivate, deliver,
collect, provision,
entertain, referee,
nurse, sanitise,
civilise, advise,
defend, bath and
put to bed the next
generation."

When your holidays come round, it's so great to get away from it all.

Holidays are just like
work. You spend your time
hanging around waiting
for lunch.

"This is the last time
I book a cheap holiday on
the internet…"

When you retire, the problem is you end up so busy.

He loved gardening.

"Remind me to stop
volunteering for things."

"I'm hoping that yoga will solve all my problems."

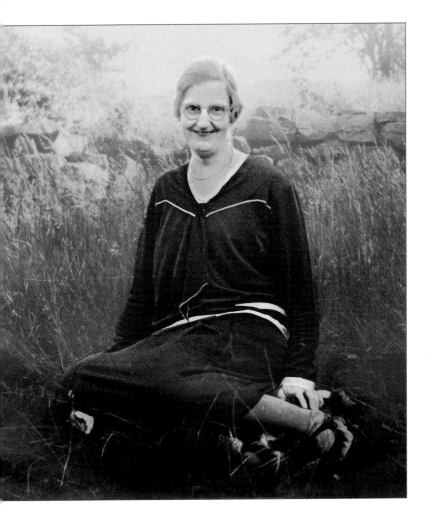

Stuff work!

Cath Tate has lived and worked in London for more years than she cares to mention. She currently runs a greetings card company, Cath Tate Cards, with her daughter Rosie: the bulk of the photos and captions in this book started life as greetings cards.

The photos have been collected over the years by Cath and her friends in junk shops and vintage fairs. They are all genuine and show people in all their glory, on the beach, on a day out, posing stiffly for the photographer, drinking with friends, smiling or scowling at the camera.

The photographs were all taken sometime between 1880 and 1960. Times change but people, their friendships, their little joys and stupid mistakes, remain the same. Some things have changed though, and Cath Tate has used modern technical wizardry to tease some colour into the cheeks of those whose cheeks lost their colour some time ago.

The quotes that go with the photos come from random corners of life and usually reflect some current concern that is bugging her.

If you want to see all the current greetings cards and other ephemera available from Cath Tate Cards see www.cathtatecards.com

Cath Tate

Many thanks to all those helped me put this book together, including Discordia, who have fed me with wonderful photos and ideas over the years, and Suzanne Perkins, who has made sure everything looks OK, and also has a good line in jokes.